Quiet Moments

✠✠✠

by

Frances L. Smith

DORRANCE PUBLISHING CO., INC.
PITTSBURGH, PENNSYLVANIA 15222

ISBN # 0-8059-5685-9
Printed in the United States of America

First Printing

For information or to order additional books, please write:
Dorrance Publishing Co., Inc.
643 Smithfield Street
Pittsburgh, Pennsylvania 15222
U.S.A.
1 800 788 7654
Or visit our web site and on-line catalog at *www.dorrancepublishing.com*

To my Sister Ethel Mae
who I felt so honored to be with as
she traveled on her journey.

✠✠✠

Contents

Preface

My life for the past years has been spent with the finest people. I had the inspiration of my parents, most especially of my mother, Frances. I also had that of my sister who was so very special in my life. We enjoyed life, and I felt privileged to be with her as she traveled on her journey. Finally, I had the love of my brother, Julius, who inspired me with his love for life. My sons, Joseph and Raymond, who made me realize what living is all about, and my granddaughter, Stephanie, also has encouraged me.

This poetry is of my own growing awareness put into words.

I can remember, as if it were yesterday, sitting with my family and friends whose heavy the obstacles, racism and sexism that could have made their route all but impossible. It brought me into a world of thought, thoughts I could put into words. I developed deeper emotions about my life and my greatest triumphs. This is my Anthology of Poems.

Love Is Free

I wonder: Have you ever stopped to think,
how poorly you might fare
if love cost you money
and you weren't a millionaire?
Be thankful then that love is free, available for every person-
then fill your heart until it runs over,
spilling just all you can.

And everywhere you let it spill
lovely flowers will start to grow.
It matters not how poor the soil
that is reached by the overflow:
Bright blooms hide the ugly
scars left on some heart
so long ago.
Love really grows the nicest flowers
this Earth will ever grow.

August 1984

Forgive and Forget

They say you must forgive and forget.
I'll agree it's the right thing to do.
Only I'm not an angel, I'm hopelessly set.
I'll forgive and remember too.

I'll forgive your breaking a vow.
Love leaves me no other choice.
Only I can't forget-I'll tell you now
the sound of your dear voice.

I'll forgive your neglect of me.
Although love knows not neglected,
Friendship does.
But I can't forget; I'll always see
the life in your eyes.

Surely I'll forgive the heartache;
for love keeps no record of such.
But I won't forget for love's sake
your hands' warm, friendly touch.

Surely I'll forgive all future wrong.
It's one of love's strange ways.
But I won't forget it's my heart's
theme song,
your faith in me those trying days.
Yes-I really am quite human.
I forgive, but I can't forget-
Maybe God has a future plan
And I will make me an angel-yet.

October 1984

2

Tell Me

Tell me: How long is forever,
when does it really end?
Is it how long we promised to remember
And love each other as friends.
Did you really mean you'd remember?
To me it was a solemn vow-
And I really meant forever.
Tell me what you really meant, now.

July 1996

Questions

Sons of Man, so many blind Christians
are serving you this way.
Can they escape the destruction
of the awful Judgement Day?

Son of God, will you answer these questions?
Will you accept such inconsistency?
May they dally now, with salvation
and still live forever with Thee?

June 1997

Always Present

I spend days, daydreaming
dreams that I hope come true.
But those dreams add to the longing
to really be with you.

And often I'm lost in memories
of times I've spent with you;
and until dreams become reality,
these memories must do.

Memories and daydreams mingling
to blueprint a future with you;
without need or dreams
or remembrance of you.

Without Dreams

Hearts without dreams are like houses without windows
and no need for doors:
there is no incentive to go out and find the
dream you never had.

Making Memories

Deliberately I'm blocking out tomorrow, thinking of today's moment
of time; for God only gives sunrise to sunset,
And tomorrow may never be mine.
So I'll make the most of each moment,
should the memory of this day be mine.

When My Ship Comes In

It's an old, old-old saying:
"I'll remember you when my ship comes in."
Folks still say it, not knowing they really have ships to come in.

Some send out ships of adventure seeking that which is not their own;
Preying on ships of another, never thinking they must some day atone.

Some send dark ships of war that forever are seeking strife with a
cargo of heartaches to trouble men sore.

They'll come drifting in at the end of life.
In mercy a few send lifeboats out,
rescuing sin-wrecked men on life's sea.

Later they'll return without a doubt,
with peace, joy, and then quality.

Yes, there are ships galore.
But it's only the wise who choose the sort of ship worth waiting for,
and always the foolish who lose.

It's an old, old-old saying:
"I'll remember you when my ship comes in."

And many say it, I'm thinking, who have sent none out to come in.

Dear Friend

I'm sending a note to remind you that taxes have taken away the
things I think most essential:
my reindeer, my work, and my sleigh
I now make my rounds on my donkey;
he is old, crippled, and slow
So you'll know if I don't see you at Christmas,
I'm out on my ass in the snow.

Christmas

When I awaken Christmas morning,
I search real well the shores of sleep
for some piece of memory,
like driftwood floating,
that I still like to keep.

December 17, 1997

My Choice

If I was truly wise, I'd pray, "Lord, let me forget, it's the easier way."
But love is all I can claim
and to forget true love would shame.
So, I will not pray this ever;
but ask instead that you remember too.

December 1997

Let Me Wait Lord

Let me stop and wait Lord,
and let my heart your leading sense;
then, stay those hurried thoughts of mine
Lest their swift pace should take me past.
The glorious vision of never-ending time.

Let me stop and wait Lord, and give you needed time
to bless Time for me to sink roots deeply
where life's true value grows,
that I might grow and reach towards you and grasp Eternity.

June 10, 1969

Candle Magic

I lived within a lonely shell.
It was gloomy and uninviting.
The paths to its door were all grass-grown,
for none came treasure seeking.

And then you walked
a grass-grown path
in idle curiosity
stepping within my lonely shell
with a candle burning brightly.

My shell's become a different place
with an air that's quite inviting.
And others walk the care for paths
since you left your candle burning.

For my sister
1967

Air Castle

And so you're busy dreaming dreams,
building our castle in the air.
And I'll bet without foundation;
For dreamers wise are very rare.

Only let me warn you, dreamer,
It's dangerous to build them so-
for they don't always fade away
Sometimes they tumble down, you know?

And though they are but the real thing
and have no weight, it's true.
If ever they came tumbling down,
they will break the heart of you.

But don't stop dreaming and building
your lonely castle in the air,
using pieces from the rubble
with hope still shining through.
Cement them well with love,
And I'm sure your dreams will come true.

Trips

Now, I have traveled many places,
but none was perfection for me.
Although I had boast of lonely things
that my travels let me see.

And then one day I took a trip;
it was short and completely free.
The perfect trip that all should take
to the foot of Calvary.

My Christmas List

I had my usual Christmas list,
With my loved one's name at the top,
and then friends as dear as family,
and new friends for whom I would shop,
with a few more faraway friends
I never from my list would drop.

And so on down to the end of the list,
writing slowly and often reluctantly.
Give this one? Well, I always have.
And this one? I should not really.
Only writing the names inflated my ego;
not many give gifts to an enemy.

And then I thought of the first Christmas gift
wrapped in swaddling clothes
God's gift came
bearing no name tag that the angels sang
and no lone soul was called by name;
just peace on Earth good will to man.
And memory bowed my head in shame.

I threw away my list
and carefully wrote another.
My Savior's name was at the top,
then all those doubtful others.
And as I wrote the last loved names,
I thought I heard angels rejoicing together.

1970

The Christmas Spirit

I am glad the spirits can't be bought
but will haunt the poorest of men.
By them a zest to life is brought,
as they haunt us time and again.

Now some of them I have learned to love
like the spirit of youth, of Spring-
while some of them bring strife and pain.

Best loved of those that haunt one's life
is the spirit of Christmas, for me
It purges hearts of self and strife; the images
of God we see. And once again it is a road,
the signs of its presence; I know it sets
men's heart attune to God,
and Christmastide lights into glass.

It permeates the very air with songs that forever will live. And one
sure sign most seem to share is the changing of "get to give."

Today its presence plainly shows; I thrill to that spirit anew that
happy people gathered together in their Christmas shopping ado.

1976

The Season's Drink

Because the season fills each cup with a vintage of the past usually,
try not to drink too deep, my friend from this cup of memory-for sadness
is at the bottom and liquids will bitter be. While happy things always float
to the top; so sip from the cup carefully and the memories of past happiness will
make your Christmas Day merry.

1982

Harvest Time

Such awful things are happening now, filling so many hearts with
fear. Gone now is the time for seeds and plow-the harvest time for Earth is here;
nations are reaping some broken word. Fierce storms and floods are so frequent
now. Our God will keep in perfect peace every heart that has stayed on him.

1980

Fellow Rider

There was many a day when we both rode the old subway,
and I did wonder if you knew who she was with her smile so friendly.
Forever we were exchanging words, and I was pleased with what I
heard. Days have slipped away into years. How many more, I thought,
know I like to question fate? So, I will ask: Is it too late?
I would really like to know: Is it late, my fellow rider?

1965

What Is Your Age

I know that you are thirty-nine, plus
And thirty-nine stands for the years.

The plus I can only guess at,
but I know it's the sum of our hopes,
dreams, and tears.

Now I pray, God will add
thirty-nine and plus more years.
in which your dreams and hopes all come true
everyday of those years for you.

1987

The World of Sound

The world of sound is a wonderful place,
and second only to the world of sight,
where one may hear matchless beauty and grace.
and the fairest whispers are fought with might.

There's the voice of enchanting spring,
meeting discordant echoes of the past.
until hope revives with growing things
to reach glad fruition at last.

Or the beauty of music-who can tell
all its beauty by word or pen?
For its voice reaches dawn where
deepest feelings dwell,
past even our own inward kin.

And always the sound of a violin works
magic in the heart of me
until I forget that the world and dreams
seem like a reality.
Numberless are the kind of voices
in this world of sound,
each special with its own power.
But for me there's no more glorious
sound than some choir magnifying
God in Song.

March 25, 1969

Wings of the Morning

I took the wings of the morning.
and flew till set of Sun,
the miles slipping like lightning-
and I was far from where pain had begun.

Winter scenes to summer change
and hope to new life sprung.
But pain too took wings that morning
I found, when my long flight was done.

August 3, 1967

In memory of my sister Ethel, who went on her journey.

Leftover Time

No time for Church Sunday for I've so many things to do-
but I'm not the only one; others stay at home on Sunday too.

No time right now for seeking God;
I'll confess to my sins later.
Just when doesn't really matter:
He's always a forgiving God.

It's the wrong time to ask me for money when I lack for my own real needs.
Right now I'll do a few good deeds and later I'll give my money.

I've no time to witness for God;
I wouldn't know how anyway,
for one must learn just what to say.
Besides, it's the preacher's place they tell me.

No time to give or pray?
No time for Church or witnessing?
But can death be told, "No time for dying;
come back--another day!"

February 1995

To Know a Wonder

If you awaken in the morning and can see, hear, and speak;
your mind is clear for thinking;
And your strength is strong,
you have all you need for reaching any goal that your heart may seek.
Don't waste a moment of this day,
for never again will it pass your way.
Your mind will cease to ponder
with the mind wrapped in slumber,
with hands and feet resting quietly.
Don't waste the moments of the day;
they are far too precious to let slip away.

1970

My Lonesome Closet

Far back as I can remember,
my closet had always been shared with
family, friend, or sister,
always for room I poorly fared.

Days, months, and even years passed by,
time seemed no change to bring.
Then one day hangers were empty,
and I had room for everything.

No longer a need for sharing,
and the closet oozed lonesomeness.
What wouldn't I give to be asking
for a hanger and room for one more dress?

Bronx, NY
August 3,1967
For Ethel Ladson, my sister

Empty Days

Far too quick tomorrow becomes our yesterday
and the things that could have been ours we have carelessly let slip away.
But no day need ever empty be if we will but look for little things,
like the friendly smile of a future friend, or a bit of joy.
May every today that comes to you be full of nice little things or one kind
word, or simply lending someone a hand for the joy it brings.

1979

Dare You

I dare not for one moment, Lord, get out
of touch with thee.
Unless evil, swift as lightning flash,
should overpower me.

Every word and act is so far reaching,
that an ounce of sin might be
bound up in the briefest moment
that's not controlled by Thee.

And only Thou and time can tell
how great my sin would be,
should I, for one brief moment,
Lord, get out of touch with Thee.

We are all like multicolored stones, dropped into
God's great ocean of time
at birth. The ripples we make
will never cease until they reach
the shores of Eternity;
where only God can judge their worth.

My Garden

My garden is a lovely place;
yet a place where anguished go,
a place still fragrant echoes haling flowers gone,
leaving weeds of sorrow to grow.
Many hours have I spent in my garden
pulling weeds, every weed I could find.
And working the soil where the seeds have been,
here planting flowers, the very choicest kind.
Then I watered my garden with tears every night.
And with laughless sunshine warmed it each day.
Someday without anguish.
I entered the gate where the bloom had hidden
scars and grief away.

1967

For my sister, Ethel Mae

The Christmas Lights

How deeply Christmas lights stir me.
Their beauty is but man-made.
How they glorify the darkness.

I see them often in the daylight,
lifeless things on buildings and trees;
dull colored gone is the beauty
we may only in darkness see.

Seeing this, I realize their beauty is not in the bulbs that we see
but a passing unseen power that man calls electricity.

And so is all the human race,
dull lifeless bulbs of varied hue
until our God sets us aglow
by his own spirit passing through.

And all through whom it is passing
glorious Earth's darkened night
with a beauty that stirs far deeper
than any Christmas light.

1976

My children have always been "The Christmas Lights."

Will I Miss You

You ask, "Will I miss you?" Yes, more than I can say.
For words are not yet coined for my feelings to convey.
But when they are, I gladly tell so very much I miss the
thrill of you through sight, sound, and touch.

But will you miss me? You ask, "Will I miss you?"
Shouldn't the question be, "If while I'm missing you,
will you remember me? To miss one who has forgotten
you, makes heartache worse, you know.
So promise you'll forget not
for I shall miss you so.

July 1984

The Touch of Spring

I had heard the sound of peepers
night after warm, damp night and
smelled spring sweet fragrances;
I sought for signs by morning light.

I saw a veil of pale green lace
spread over the mountain's side,
laced with a dogwood in bloom
lovely enough for a bride.

While in the valley, April gold
edged the door and yards far and near
with forsythia and yellow daffodils
a wiser heart it would cheer.

Green velvet was spread lavishly
over hills and open fields
It is only the touch of spring,
the earth: Such beauty it yields.

March 1978

Silent Years

After I've listened through silent years
through friendship old and new,
to hear the three most precious words
soft spoken in tones that rang true.
After tempted to accept a sham, knowing they too
in time grow few.
But I never could stand a voice off key,
and maybe, my ears have been at fault too.

Silence is not always golden; sometimes it can be really ugly, especially
when a word could exonerate a person or cheer a lonely heart.

1982

The Fourth Monkey

There are three little monkeys that we see
with eyes, ears, and lips guarded well:
a warning to the inner me, no evil to see, hear, or tell.

It's a quaint old Chinese warning,
incomplete as things human must be.
For the key to the symbol is lacking,
that warns the inner me.

There should be a fourth little monkey
with its head buried as if in thought,
thinking to warn me as God says, "As thou thinkest, thou art."

1985

Countless

Countless the memories we are making
everyday that we live and love; our minds are the tape of which we are record-
ing the power that plays them after we never leave memories behind.
Try as we will, they are always there too often.

May 1984

Last Bequest

It matters not how poor we seem when crossing
life's last great divider.
We still leave something to bequest for both friend and foe
upon this side.

It may be something that's best forgotten, or something to
hold very dear.
For every thought, each word, and each act, are in its making
while we are here.

We bequest it to all and even to few.
It's shared by everyone we have known,
the memories that form acquainceship have grown.

1983

Success

Success-a goal reached-but first we had to dream a bit
and hope a lot.

Hope is made up of two ingredients-desire and expectation-
and when both are deep and strong enough, we will work hard enough to attain it.

December 1969

Author Unknown

There are so many lovely thoughts I have found in praise and rhyme that
have stirred my heart.
While searching my soul, I read them from time to time.

How gladly I would say thank you to poets of each lovely rhyme.
But so often I found author unknown;
so my thanks must wait until the end of time.

November 1975

Wishing You Happy Birthday

There are so many special days
with ways and ways, so many ways.
to celebrate-congratulate; but none of these seem right to me.
Yours needs originality.

I could wish you so many things; and wish I do
if wishing brings the things I really want for you.
All life's nice things I will name a few-
friends galore, success, and a long, healthy life that's happy.
I know at time wishing won't come true,
but these things I wish for you.

1969

Bird Apartments

Birds have high rise apartments in the evergreen trees,
those living poles that sway in the breeze.
All kinds of birds find safe shelter there
since there's no feather-color questionnaire.
Many wait their chance
In the nearby trees for the rare unexpected vacancies.
And their twitters of contentment make such pleasant
sounds and there's need of an interpreter.
There's the mocking bird, for he sings all their songs;
I know, for I have heard.

1975

Fifty Years

Fifty full years of wedded life:
few are blessed to reach this goal.
So much to reminisce about:
the good and the bad, that which made the whole, filled
with the nicest things, enough to crowd
unpleasant things out.
giving so much to remember about.

My In-Laws
1978

We never leave memories behind; try as we will, they are always there.

Walls

Give me a tent, one room, or a cottage;
even a castle fair; it matters not which one it is
if a friend but dwells with me there.

For walls that shelter only me,
though they have all the wealth of earth,
are empty as a last year's nest and of no earthy worth.

It is sad God's Word dwells alone
and happy the soul that can boast
both walls and friend to own.

November 1969

Confession and Prayer

How many times I can't recall.
I failed to say that I know you,
but when alone, the tears of shame would fall.
No need to ask, "Lord, is it I?"
I was ashamed to call your name.
Knowing no other would do,
humbly I knelt confessing all,
crying, "Lord, forgive, it is I"

Lord, let me live this day
that at its close, these questioning words
to thee I need not say:
Lord, is it I-Lord is it I?
Not just this day, but everyday
may no wrong act, no thoughtless words
of mine. Your trust in me betray
that I may truly say it is not I today.

I believe everyone in his own heart
knows whether or not he has betrayed his Lord.
And when we ask is it,
it is an open confession of guilt
and we already know the answer.
My poems are like an autobiography of
my life and the thoughts of the real me.

April 1976

Friendship

The bridge of friendship is a beautiful thing
when completed, but quite the reverse when left unfinished.

It's a thing that must be worked on from both ends.
Many things can work, hinder, even stop:
Family, job, and distance of course; the
mailman or telephone can help work from
slowing down and stopping completely
by putting a stone or two in place.
To work in each waits for the other to
return, it is sad for that to happen.
Then there are the completed bridges we
let fall into disrepair; and we
wonder, do we dare cross them?

Small Things

Small things that pass so quick:
A glance-a smile-a word-a touch-
or a whiff of haunting fragrance-only
who keeps records of such?
Yet memory will retain them
and make of them so much.

Remembering Familiar Things

With the sight of lonely callalillies comes
a sense of familiar things.
The tall blue spears of delphiniums the same
familiar feelings bring.

Red tulips, a long-stem medium
red rose, whatever lonely that my eyes see,
the grace of the wind-blown willows.
All are reminders, even now that sweet
fragrance on the breeze.

Then some new scent that seems familiar
or hearing a voice now silent in another song,
The past invades the present;
I wonder, will it be for long?

Thoughts of my sister, Ethel, I still love dearly.

July 1982

Time Is Priceless

Each bit of time I spend with you
is like a precious jewel that's added
to my string of memories,
worth more to me than real jewels
could ever be.
And there's no need to insure them to keep them safe from thieves.
For I keep this priceless string of jewels.
Deep in the heart of me.

August 1987

Real Treasure

The ship I sent seeking treasure
has never yet come in
and nothing else I try
ever seems to win.
But there are some things money
can't buy.
And these are the things that I wish for you.
Set the sails to the wind of faith
and pray faithfully long enough, someday
they will come true.

September 1994

My Shadow

Now I have a lonely shadow,
memories of a dear distant friend.
And everywhere I chance to go,
from sunrise to day's end,
these memories always follow
until sleep comes and the shadows end.
There can be no shadows without the
sunshine of friendship's love.

March 1984

Flying My Thoughts

So many thoughts I just breathed in the air,
wordless thoughts a sort of prayer,
hoping they will land where the need is great.

No matter where-but not too late
to ease the heavy load of someone
walking life's rough road.
And should they drift over the seas,
may they help an asking heart to ease.
Or bring new hope to one whose
mind is seeking a new way to find
real peace, in a happier future time.
May God speed all these thoughts of mine.

1964

Quick to Hang Up

When I called God on the prayer phone,
I talked continuously, telling him in pleading tones
how I thought certain things should be and
all that I needed for my own.
And then hung up so he could answer me.

June 1980

Inseparable Things

What is spring without its song birds,
summer without the flowers, fall
without bright foliage, and winter
without snow showers?

What is the night without stars and the day
without moonlight; the day without
a shining sun or day's end without
a sunset or lovely rose dawns
as the day begun?

What is the flower without fragrance.
or birds robbed of their song; a brook
without laughing water, or
empty woods when the wild life's gone.

What is Christmas without giving or
an Easter without gala array?
All these things are like lives
without hope of a future day:
Joyous words without joyous music.

January 1985

Understanding

I buried heartbreak and sorrow,
all my plans for the future years.
And I wondered if such things
ever grow
as I watered them with my tears.

The days grew to months, and years went by.
Then a friend's sympathy needed.
Sadly, thoughts came back with a sigh
where my grief laid deeply buried.
And I found such things really grow,
producing true understanding.
And my whispered words brought
"I know";
they knew that I still was remembering.

August 1967

Excuse and Regret

If I had known you had not longed to live,
I would not have tarried by the way
A poor excuse this is if we use it so often
and needs so little thought for us to say.

Since God does not confide in man,
no one another's length of days can say;
and knowing this, I must with sad regrets abide
My every future day.

1968

Beauty for Ashes

I wonder, have you ever thought
(It's a source of wonder to me.)
how first some evil must wrought wherever some beauty can be?

There can be no rainbow
until after clouds and rain.
Never does God's healing ever flow until the channel
is dug by pain.

And where is the need for pardon,
before we have transgressed in sin?
And the prize is never given until after we strive and win.

And only to those who have loved and lost
comes the joy of finding again.
And yes the pain we some can cast
wherever we bring came the list seem almost unending.
It's exhausted my gift of rhyme
And still without my explaining for the story is really divine.

Best, if you never yet have thought,
think now and thankful be
that out of the evils Satan has brought
God still works beauty for harmony.

Tumbleweed

As drifting over the desert sands,
someone saw a beauty in you,

and wrote a song of the freedom many wish they knew,

And then he saw the weed one day,
a prickly and unfriendly thing,
tumbling along in the wind really free.

And I too felt that song, an urge to sing.

1993

Lonely Stations

I have been so often to the station
to welcome friends or bid farewell
without a thought for the lonely ones
who so silently came and went.
Then one day I was all alone
without a person to care.
where in the world had I come from
or where in the world I went.

No outstretched hand and glad hello,
no one to bid me a fond farewell,
so glad you came, or must you go
at journey beginning and end.
I never thought, it would happen to me,
and its happening to me made me sad.
Until, I remembered I wasn't alone:
God never forgot a friend.

1964

Just an Atom

When you feel life is against you
and heaven seems dark above,
just drop an atom of pure faith into the
rich soil of love.
Then, watch the miracles happen-things
you never dreamed of.

1999

Special Days

Surely everyone must hold
one day above the rest;
So not a cloudy day or clear
but someone loves it best.
Loves it just because that day
they first met someone dear
Or just because the record says
a loved life started here.

Freedom Day for an eager lad
Just turning twenty-one,
while on the fourth a nation's
glad over Independence won.

The reasons are as myriad as
the beauty hearts of men,
affecting one or millions as the
occasion might have been.

Could there be a day so fraught
With meaning for all men?
That every man, if he was taught
Would loves allegiance lend?

With doubt, I search the calendar
for one, just one such day.
And found one wonder of wonders
that Resurrection Day.

April 1982

Another Chance

Each breath I draw
is another chance to whisper,
"Dear Lord, forgive,"
then, once more start again.

Each step I take-
a chance to walk from sin,
seeking God's forgiveness and
His peace within.

Each thought-a chance
to lift my soul toward God
as I wearily toil
beneath life's relentless rod.

Each is a chance to hear
and hearken to his word
with my desire to read the things
I have not heard.

If I can count each breath,
each step, each thought
each word I hear and read,
then can I count each chance
God gives me
a better life to lead.

December 1970

Another Chance

I heard those words once long ago
and wondered do we get that chance.
Then years later another spoke; then
It was then I knew--sometimes
Yes, sometimes No.

The most precious gift one can give
another is a moment of their time
another chance to prove themselves
Who knows which one will benefit the most?

The Perfect Gift

So many times I have tried to give the perfect gift, you know.
But always when the gift arrived, discrepancies would show
even although I had chosen with great care
since I cared for the one to whom it would go.
Then I thought of the perfect gift
God sent so long ago
And knew that any gift of mine
must imperfection show.

After years of trying to give the perfect gift, this is true.

1969